Ephemeral Earth

Radha Subramaniam

Writersgram
Publications

Ephemeral Earth
by Radha Subramaniam

First Impression: October 2021

© Radha Subramaniam

ISBN: 978-93-5485-401-9

Published by: Writersgram Publications, New Delhi

www.writersgram.com
publications@writersgram.com

Dedication

To our planet, and to all those who
believe Global Warming is real.

Contents

Preface

This book is the result of rare moments of lucidity and more frequently, moments of frustrating inability to put into words, thoughts and feelings so strange and wonderous, I have taken to questioning my sanity. Never before have I let my subconscious be my only guiding light or let my pen charter my course through dark corridors of thought, with no intervention from reasoned argument, as I have with this short compilation of a select few poems I treasure.

As is the case with many of us who write, there are certain thoughts which come to me as I go about my day which I will write down because I am rarely parted from pen or paper. These thoughts sometimes wither away but more often than not, they take root, burst into bloom, and mature into trees laden with fruit; each fruit different, every experience momentous, yet fleeting, in this vast realm of multiple realities.

Through the course of writing these poems, I have rediscovered a part of myself long buried under a myriad of mundane, everyday chores. In every sense of the word, I write, because I crave the cathartic release I only experience when I let my consciousness spill onto paper. I encourage everyone who reads this book to revisit things they would like to pick up again, be it art, music, or like me, simply putting pen to paper and dreading the outcome.

Introduction

A mote of dust suspended in a sunbeam is how Carl Sagan refers to planet earth in his book, 'A Pale Blue Dot: A Vision of the Human Future in Space'.

As I began inking thoughts on paper, I could not help but think of our insignificance as a species in this vast cosmos. This lifetime is but a sojourn, a fleeting luxury, like rain in the desert or wildflowers in summer, both instances which I elaborate on, in the poems 'Land Without End' and 'A Summer Serenade'. Each poem in this book derives inspiration from the earth and while some poems like 'River of Ink' and 'Grey Rainbows' speak extensively about social issues such as racial inequality and societal constructs which allow for such discrimination to perpetuate, through each poem runs a common vein connecting us to the earth, for to speak of one is to speak of the other; unified, yet in essence divided.

I speak of the heedless destruction of the earth's forests, and the devastating consequences, if the size of our carbon footprint continues to grow in the poem 'Black Gold.' I also touch upon the economic and cultural divide within human society which makes it difficult to work towards a sustainable future in the poems 'City Lights' and 'Forest for the Trees'.

Poems like 'The Harvest Queen' and 'Green Sea Turtle' wax eloquent on how every transient occurrence in nature holds its own, whereas the poems 'Oblivion' and 'Stolen Dreams' reflect on the fragility of human life.

Earth itself will someday cease to exist and though such an occurrence is beyond our lifetimes, our planet is but ephemeral when we equate it to the incomprehensible vastness of the universe. This book is a collection of prose, which encourages readers to think beyond the individual and of the collective consciousness. Each poem of course, is also open to interpretation since no individual will think like another and to expect that will be nothing short of narcissism.

"For small creatures such as we the vastness is bearable only through love."

Carl Sagan

Acknowledgement

My journey through the realms of stories and poetry has never been uneventful. In fact, it is what seems like a never-ending, marvellous cycle of reading one book, while waiting to begin the next. I owe a lot of who I am today, to the books that shaped me and also to those that did not make a lasting impression.

I am indebted to my mother, who is the strongest woman I know. She has weathered every storm with impeccable grace, while being a constant source of encouragement and a pillar of strength. I inherit from her my passion for writing and my type A personality. I am also grateful to have a father who I love dearly, for his unflinching, albeit misplaced belief in the fact that I am capable of doing anything I set my heart to, and a brother, without whose continued support and sense of humour, my life would be despondent. I am also eternally grateful to my husband, who has stood by me through thick and thin. He is the most wonderful man I know and yet I am thankful he is not in charge of coming up with titles for my books. I would also like to acknowledge my source of ceaseless inspiration, my grandmother, who taught me that the earth is a treasure we must cherish. She also taught me that women can do whatever they want to do, whenever they want to do it. I thank my very large family, for showing me that we can all be different and yet, we can always share love, hugs, and laughs.

I must also acknowledge my friends, who are always willing to lift me up when I need them to. I owe you much, for your constant ability to validate my existence and my sense of humour.

I thank my cat, Georgie, who has been a constant source of warmth and comfort through all the long nights and has left far more indelible impressions on me than words ever will.

Lastly, I acknowledge the remarkably efficient team of Writersgram Publications, without whom, this work of literary genius would not be possible.

The Harvest Queen

Dawn casts her golden glow,
Over tranquil waters below.
A red squirrel looks askance,
As elusive sunbeams dance.
Light suffuses the mist rising from the lake
A Luminous, shimmering haze.
The midday sky was a brilliant blue;
The canopy shone in every hue.
The leaves have shed their verdant green,
For a burnished red, and orange sheen.
A radiant bouquet,
Oh, such a glorious autumnal display.
Dusk settles in over peaks and valleys;
Red maple and aspen sway,
As a crisp fall breeze, carries fallen leaves away.
The last rays of sunlight,
Dapple the forest floor in gold,
A breathtaking sight to behold.
As dusk fades into a moonlit night,
A flock of wild geese take flight,
As the silvery light of the moonbeams shone,
Autumn reigns resplendent on her silver
gossamer throne.
Until lady frost is back in town,
The harvest queen shall wield her crown.

We Dream In Purple

Dusk sweeps across the rolling hills,
Over lavender fields, and enchanting glades,
A fine mist hangs over verdant valleys,
As the last of the light fades.

Beneath a byzantine sky,
Soft as velvet,
Till morning is nigh,
We dream in purple,
You and I.

Tread softly on damp grass,
Wildflowers, in lilac bloom,
An indigo bunting flies by,
Dispelling purple gloom.

Amethyst robes gleaming in starlight,
Deep in slumber we lie,
On a dark, warm summers night,
We dream in purple,
You and I.

Look through the mirror and you shall see,
An everlasting ocean lies beyond,
Swim across infinity
And you, can always be found.

Soft light filters through diaphanous drapes,
And spreads across a mulberry sky,
And even though we are now awake,
We dream in purple,
You and I.

Black Gold

Flames ravage her tresses,
Ash rains down,
From scorching, oppressive skies
Battle scarred and bone weary,
Will she rise?

Fissures dissect her glacial heart,
She breaks from deep within,
Ever receding,
And over her battered, bruised skin,
We drown in sanguine flood.

Silent screams,
Pierce the moonless night,
Broken body and shattered soul,
Her blood glistens,
Black Gold.

Birds take flight over a red horizon,
Tornadoes sweep across the barren countryside,
Men boasting ruthless conquests,
Green changing hands,
Over a lifeless land.

An unforgiving tide ebbs and flows,
And speaks of all her sorrows,
When we struggle to breathe,
And if there will be no morrow,
She will still rise.

River of Ink

He carried it in his heart,
It slowly tore him apart.
On his head a heavy crown,
In his secrets he would drown.

He dragged his feet,
And beat his chest,
For a man so wretched,
There was no rest.

Sword or scale?
Words pierce him like a lance,
Poison or pen?
A frenzied dance.

He cries a river of ink,
This ravaged man,
Parched throat,
And yet he wrote.

Words poured from his heart,
And set him free,
This river of ink from bleeding hand,
Wound its way through all the land.

It speaks a tongue of truth and lies,
It speaks of suffering and joy alike,
He built a bridge across this river of ink,
As his bejeweled crown began to sink.

Summer Serenade

Legs dangling off my perch,
On a cloudless summer day,
Toes grazing the cool surface of the lake,
I feel the breeze in my hair,
And hear the sounds of summer,
In the dulcet tunes of songbirds,
Perched on fragrant magnolia trees,
The gently rustling leaves,
And the buzzing of the bees.
I watch the blue skies,
Face upturned to catch the sun's rays,
On summer days like these.
Days of endless sunshine,
A riot of colours,
Fields and fields of wildflowers.
I run barefoot through green grass,
And skip stones off lakes clear as glass,
And after an eternity,
Deep in the glade,
The crickets start to serenade,
The songs of summers past,
And those yet to come.
I walk past glowing fireflies,
The remnants, of summers light.

The Time Traveller

Tick tock goes the clock,
A shimmer in the air.
A gleam of cloak and glimmer of skin,
A sudden click of the lock.
He wears a sheath of times long past,
And around him slithers a serpentine future,
He will most certainly outlast.
Both beautiful and terrible all at once,
His footsteps fall like soft velvet.
He looks defeated today,
And yet, as sprightly as he was yesterday.
As he looks down upon a sleeping figure,
Who he knows will tomorrow, be led astray.
He could shake him awake,
Show him the way,
For he has seen the unseen,
And all that lies in between.
So, he stands with his hand outstretched,
For he is not prepared for the consequences.
He knows everything and can do naught,
In this infinite loop of time, he is caught.
Free to travel to boundless dimensions,
And yet a prisoner of his own invention.

City Lights

Stilettos on marble floors,
Heavy brass knockers,
On polished oak doors.
Carpeted hallways and plush armchairs,
Men in suits, debonair.

They play charades,
Seated on plush Persian rugs,
Beside crackling flames,
In an ornate fireplace,
Sipping hot cocoa in porcelain mugs.

She lies still on frozen ground;
Soft snow clung to her eyelashes,
When her emaciated body was found.
As they stood on snow, stained red,
A dime a dozen they said.

They play charades,
Where ramshackle houses abound.
In decrepit alleyways,
They run barefoot,
On needle strewn ground.

A stained veneer,
Vacant smiles and hollow hearts,
Bleeding green.
Skyscrapers and silhouettes,
City lights,
Iridescent, pearly white.

Shoebox

I open the lid and peer in,
Dust motes in sunbeams,
I walk a path I have walked before,
Towards a beckoning, familiar shore.

I was but all of four,
And standing on tippy toes,
Trying to catch a feather floating by,
When you plucked it from the sky,
And pressed it into my little hand.

I was but all of eight,
Building a castle from soft sand,
I found a little red button,
From a far away, distant, land?

And soon after when I was ten,
I pressed this little flower,
Between the pages of a book,
A secret, within the fold,
One that was mine to hold.

Then when I was sixteen,
I tucked away a treasured gift,
A tangible link,
to memories we once lived.

Raindrops on windowpanes,
Chasing waves,
Footprints on the sands of time,
And as time flew by,
Gone, in the blink of an eye.

Trinkets and Talismans,
Lost years,
Only to be found,
Time and time again,
Like petrichor,
In a shoebox.

Summer Blues

Blue is the colour of the Summer Sky,
Sunny days and Warm Nights.
A balmy breeze blows from the west,
Gently swirling around your blue summer dress.
Blue eggs in a robin's nest,
Wildflowers and deep lakes.
Mighty oceans, fathoms deep,
And in those depths, do creatures creep,
Scales gleaming gold and blue and green.
Blue waves, frosted white,
Crashing onto soft sand,
Where you left footprints,
Once upon a time
When the blue moon shone high,
In a midnight blue sky.
The blue jay sings a tune so sweet,
As a summer breeze wafts through the trees,
And far away in a tropical land,
A blue Macaw takes flight.
Spread your wings, feather light,
For summer is here, my dear.
Shake away those blues,
Feel the warmth in your bones,
And a spring in your step,
As you paint the town,
In summer hues,
For Summer is my only muse.

Forest for the trees

Listen to the sounds of the sea,
Feel the earth move,
Let the air breathe.
Watch the moving shadows,
Let still waters flow.

A new star is born,
And celestial bodies move,
Let the walls cave in
Let the battle begin,
For the army lies within.

Feel your heart beating,
As the river meets the sea,
The reason why there is a rainbow, after a storm.
There is a world in the skies and a world in the seas,
Can't you see the forest for the trees?

I see you with my eyes closed,
There's magic right here,
Feel it pulse through your veins,
Let the sound of life carry you through,
Let courage override your fear.

Can you feel the beat?
Hear the victory march?
The sound of a hundred feet.
Open your doors,
And you will find your way home.

Solivagant

Vast plains blanketed in soft grass,
They stretch beyond what I can see.
Where the sky meets the earth,
The ocean beckons,
And I walk across this boundless expanse,
With its vales and valleys,
Arches and alleys.
Snowflakes melt,
As I catch them in the palm of my hand.
An evanescent moment,
Frozen in time, an enduring memory.
The sun rises and sets,
I traverse the seas,
Holding secrets in their depths,
A glint of scale and glitter of fin,
Rolling waves that pull me in.
Under a million stars,
And galaxies beyond my reach,
I forge my path,
Across snowy peaks.
I hear my heartbeat, as I climb,
Insignificant, yet profound.
Through an infinite loop,
Of space and time.

Slow Burn

A heavy fog obscures my vision,
A consuming Cimmerian darkness,
Static blares from a stereo,
In an apathetic world.
Bodies writhe in the dark,
Blinded by what they cannot see,
Shallow breath on frosted glass,
As his vision fades.
A slow burn,
A spark ignites,
It grows into a raging flame,
Feeding on our shame.
We can see the light,
If only we open our eyes,
Tonight, we are unfettered,
Tomorrow we shall be free.
I raise my hand,
I strike a match,
I set fire to the storm inside,
And jump into the rising tide.
Hope shines bright in your eyes,
As we look up at the burning skies.

Land Without End

It stretches far beyond your reach,
This land without end.
An unforgiving sun beats down,
Over a mercurial landscape.
Brazen in its barrenness,
A desolate beauty,
Whose undulating dunes,
Stretch across an empty horizon.
Old bones lay weary,
Every glistening oasis a mirage,
The wind blows tumbleweed,
Across parched land,
In the vast emptiness
Between earth and space,
As the stars rise,
Over sparkling grains of sand.
The dunes rise and fall,
As the wind moves the earth,
Weather-beaten and devoid of grace.
This forsaken land spares none at all,
Hollow cheeks and sunken eyes,
I was a lonely traveller who lost my way,
Among the few who lived to tell this tale,
For I was blessed with desert rain.
Someday when I shall close my eyes,
To look beyond the silken veil,
And fall into a final sleep,
Lay me to rest on golden sand,
My heart this windswept land shall keep.

Conch Shell

I hear the sound of the waves,
I smell salt in the air,
And feel the wind in my hair.
I walk on soft sand,
And leave footprints on land.
I watch the waves break,
I watch them recede,
Taking with them shells and twigs,
Sand and seaweed.
As I lower the conch shell from my ear,
Silence prevails.
It is Profound and deafening,
Leaving nothing in its wake.
I return to the present,
With a smile on my face,
For when I have to escape for a while,
All I need to do is close my eyes.
We have memories of the place we belong to you
see,
This conch shell, and me.

Green Sea Turtle

As waves crash onto white beaches,
The tide crests and falls,
Turtle hatchlings wade toward the ocean,
Silver bodies under a moonlit night.
They clamber through sand,
And plunge into the fray,
Borne on the swelling tide,
Carried far away from land.
Tiny flippers cut through the waves,
And soon they are gone from sight.
I almost turn and walk away,
When I see one break the surface.
She takes her first sea borne breath,
Before wading into the green gloom,
With deft elegance and grace.
Embarking on a journey,
Into the depths of the unknown,
Amid forests of dark seaweed,
And coral of every colour,
To propel herself through oceanic currents,
And sing the songs of the sea.
Maybe I shall see her again someday,
When she changes course,
For she will return,
To the place where she was born.
I see flippers on white sand,
As she begins wading inland.

Grey Rainbows

Rain clouds blanket a colourless world,
As storms chase us across oceans.
Ships sink anchors on a broken harbour,
What looked so whole from afar,
Broken from within.
A bleak sun sets over parched land,
Flimsy walls stretch westward.
Hold your bleeding heart in your hand,
The memory of a hug lingers,
As we melt into shadows.
A bridge is built, only to burn,
Time and time again we break,
A deep, gut wrenching ache,
Every breath is agony.
We watch from the fringes of humanity,
As the light fades from your eyes.
In the calm after the storm,
We see a grey rainbow across a pallid sky,
And then we step into the light.
As we cease to whisper,
But begin to speak,
Each life is a splendid story,
See every colour in all its glory.
A path carved in bone and blood,
Every tear a sacred flood,
And when this tempest has passed us by,
Every caged bird will fly.
We see an arch of varied hue,
And a new dawn will rise anew.

The Sound of Silence

Do you hear your heart beating?
The rhythmic beat resounding.
Feel the blood flowing through your veins,
Your lungs contracting and expanding.
Do you hear your breath whooshing?
You strain your ears,
Can you hear the sound of silence?
It comes in thundering waves,
As it engulfs and enslaves.
Your heart starts to beat faster,
And your breath is stolen away.
Suffocating under powerful currents,
As they lead you astray.
Can you see the rocky outcrop?
A jagged shoreline in sight.
Listen to your clamoring thoughts,
You cannot give up without a fight.
When silence pulls you down deeper,
Allow your voice to take flight.
Wield courage like a weapon,
And you shall see the light.
When you struggle to breathe,
Use silence as your shield.
If you can only hear one voice,
Let it speak.

Dying Embers

In the eye of the storm we stand,
This is where it all began.
A spark in the darkest night,
A flicker,
A flame,
You could not tame.

It had taken root in her heart,
Famished,
Starved,
It devoured all in its path.
Until you couldn't see the dawn,
For the towering inferno beyond.

Scalding, raging,
A fiery wrath.
Smouldering,
Undying.
Till Conqueror became the conquered,
And the Vanquished were unshackled.

The fiery beast,
Consumed all within reach.
When all but the stars in the sky remained,
We saw charred earth,
beneath our feet.

Her blackened heart, bleeding red,
It was too late to weep.
For those glowing,
Dying embers,
That is all we have,
To remember.

Before Dawn

The sun rises with you,
When it sets with me.
Some people open doors,
And we build windows,
To watch the world pass by.
It takes a while to figure out,
How funny life can be.
It is a parody of what is real,
Of what could have been.
We count minutes and live days,
We may walk together, or part ways.
Walking miles, in the dark,
Will we get there, before dawn?
Though the sun sets with you,
And rises with me,
Maybe someday,
We shall see,
Change can be constant,
And the universe infinite.

Stolen Dreams

They come for you,
Treading soft and light,
Into the deep, dark, night.
They emerge from the shadows,
Reeking of despair,
Cold hands, on clammy skin,
You try to still your racing heart,
But they steal your dreams,
To tear them apart.
They silence your screams,
As terror keeps you shackled,
And your eyes shut tight,
Surrender to the oblivion without a fight,
For then you shall feel no pain,
Or surely, you must drown in shame.
Your heart now beats in vain,
As despair drags you down,
A great, dark sleep beckons,
You strain to hold on, to firm ground.
Through the heavy silence,
Can you hear a voice calling your name?
You reach out through the oppressive gloom,
The heavy chains fall away,
And a glimmer of hope holds darkness at bay.
You spread your wings as you see the light,
For ahead lies a dazzling new day,
Feel the wind in your hair as you take flight,
Chasing stolen dreams,
Through a deep, dark night.

After the flood

The storm clouds part,
To reveal clear skies,
In its wake a pervasive silence,
Heavy with a thousand cries.

Raging rivers split at the seams,
Now recede into streams,
The rain has abated,
Her bloodlust now sated.

Through a once fertile soil,
Deep furrows etched,
And all the men who toil,
Now lie wretched.

Bleeding rivulets meet the sea,
As the mighty crown fell,
She brings every man to his knee,
And death shall ring his knell.

Ink bleeds into murky waters,
Every written word a lie,
As a lamb is led to slaughter,
Under a remorseless sky

The Jackdaw

Perched atop the prickly briar,
The Jackdaw's curious eye catches mine,
Solemnly, he sits on his perch,
A frequent visitor, a friendly sign.

I watch him from the window,
As he swoops down onto the lawn,
Methodically scouring the grass,
For sustenance, early this dawn.

We spend the day in companionable silence,
I watch him preen his glossy feathers,
As I sit out on my porch to read,
And he pecks at scattered birdseed.

When the light starts to fade,
He bade me goodbye,
As he flew over the glade,
To his nest in the spire.

I peep through the dew drenched glass,
Yet again when I wake to the early light of dawn,
I see him perched on the briar,
And then my heart sings as I put the kettle on.

Bed of Roses

They walk barefoot,
On scorching concrete,
In the sweltering heat.
The children walked beside them,
In shoes too big for their feet.

Many miles they walk,
In torn clothes,
Their feet cracked,
Lips parched,
Faces haggard.

Emaciated bodies,
A drop in the ocean.
Voices pleading,
None shall pause,
Swept away by thunderous applause.

As rose petals fall,
From the skies,
Scarlet as the bloody footsteps,
On unholy ground.
Entrenched in secrets and lies.

They gasp and stagger,
Defeated, by thirst and hunger.
No tears are shed,
For those that are left behind,
In eternal slumber.

The sickly smell of rotting flesh fills the air,
A tiny silhouette,
Crouches beside skeletal remains,
Of a once tender touch,
Like a long-forgotten lullaby.

Unseeing eyes look skyward,
As the sun sets over this condemned land,
Unshed tears leave no tracks,
As the lifeless form reposes,
On a bed of scarlet roses.

Oblivion

Memories fall through the cracks,
A slow spiral towards oblivion,
As you watch the world go by,
Beneath an April blue sky.

Familiar faces appear out of focus,
A fine mist settles over green grass,
A warm touch on your shoulder,
Someone you instantly remember.

And so you shake it off,
When you lose your way to work,
You were just out of tune,
That early morning in June.

You try to paint a once vivid memory,
Your mind like a blank canvas,
Just like the red maple in Fall,
With no colour at all.

Like lost pieces in a Christmas puzzle,
Never to be found,
It's on the tip of your tongue,
A song that she always sung.

Young leaves shall usher in spring,
And a verdant summer shall follow,
The ash loses its leaves again this autumn,
A barren winter on the morrow.

As you look out of the window,
You feel a warm touch on your shoulder,
Someone you cannot remember,
This cold, gray December.

Icarus

Parched earth,
Teetering on a precipice,
Flames leap and dance
Engulfing the sky

Colossal tidal waves,
Sweep cities away,
As the permafrost melts,
And the mighty glacier retreats

A Labyrinth of fire and Ice,
Teeming with life,
Under a cloak of virtue and vice,
Eternal Strife.

Our lungs on fire,
We fall as Icarus fell,
Broken waxwork,
Into the abyss

A phoenix will rise,
As the forests burn,
Ashes to ashes,
We will always return.